THE

BOOK

WRITE BLOODY PUBLISHING
NASHVILLE, TN

A publication of Write Bloody Publishing, Nashville, TN

Book design by Nathan Warkentin.
Type set in Stempel Garamond and Pointedly Mad.

Edited by Write Bloody Publishing.

www.writebloody.com
www.electricwhale.com

"ALL BOOKS ARE CHILDREN'S BOOKS...
IF THE KID CAN READ."

-MITCH HEDBERG

TABLE OF
CONTENTS

PROLOGUE

ANIS MOJGANI

BUDDY WAKEFIELD

THEE GALA TALE OF SOLOMON SPARROW

Seadogs and scalawags, maidens and minions, gals and gales, this the final letter left by the last in the long line of Solomon Sparrow's. If you do indeed choose to navigate the seas of these words, to tie square knots to the masts of this letter and open her sails to the wind, then pull your aching bones closer and gander at these waters, lest your own heart be judged.

In the letter below you will find the tale of a waterlogged boy, the story of whales with the skin of a jellyfish, and the unnerving account of a heartless sea captain who searched the misty oceanas for love and passion but found only emptiness and grief. Land lubbers and savvy peg leggers, ye are best advised to snag a pitcher of cold ale and to read this letter in the light of day for these words and this story are not for the weak of knees or the faint of heart!

TO MY FIVE ESTEEMED HEIRS, by Mr. Sparrow

If you are each reading this letter then my time as Solomon Sparrow IX has come to an end. My gnarled body and sea worn skin have withered to a heatless heap. My thick knuckles will fall heavy only the wheel of the ocean and never again on the wheel of my great fleet of ships. These words are my final sound bellowing from the foghorn of my lungs, a cry to all the ships coasting near these shores and calling them to huddle at the docks and gather to launch my funeral pyre out toward the horizon.

To you my heirs I have left you each a single gift and a single simple task. However, before I tell ye of this gift and unveil the details of this task I must first tell the tale of how all Solomon Sparrow's came into possession of the great item that my death now delivers to you.

My boys, my five gentle and ridiculous boys, let me tell you that our ability to love comes from the ocean. The ocean is a vast beauty and her heart pounds with the life of beings and creatures that most landlubbers could never create in their wildest of imaginations! The ocean is so grand, we become small and finite next to her.

Aye, but this sense of something so large surrounding our little universe in a way never visited dock or port. The crew of The Maiden Voyage did not know land and longed only for the endless distances. These slimy scalawags knew only the ocean. These seadogs ate and drank from the ocean, built bookshelf and table from the bones spit up onto their deck.

From the corners of the boats bowels the boy watched in wonder as men with harpoon arms feasted on the wet bowels of whales, as women with fish for lips made love to sea captains with eyeless faceless and toothless grins. Girls fiddled violins with dagger fingers, boys itched their starfish kneecaps. Each evening feasts of jellyfish and sea lions were flopped on the tables of alabaster whalebones. The crew swigged the blood of these creatures, cut them at the bowels and consumed their guts. At the end of each feast the crew would fall silent and a man who the boy could not see would lift a single jellyfish in the air and cut it lengthwise. From the jellyfish a circus of lights and fireworks ignited. At this, the crew would fling open their jowls and drink the sputtering jellyfish guts as they shot from the sky like falling stars. After all of the jellyfish had been consumed the crew gathered at the deck edge to gaze at the water and long for long lost lovers.

What drew the boy from his refuge was not the men with harpoons for arms or the boys with pistol fingers nor was it the women with slimy tentacles springing from their shoulders. Not even the pretty girl whose body grew out from the bow of the ship and who's eyes were filled with two oceans that no man or woman would ever sail could convince the boy to come onto the deck.

What took him this evening was a glance through the cracks in the deck boards. The boy felt his syringe thin veins pique at the sight of a captain whose chest held a crater in the shape of a human heart. The loose skin on the captain's chest fluttered in the sea breeze, a set of weary and weathered sails worn from the man's search for a dock that he never found. Possessed by this vision, the boy staggered out of the ship's bowels and onto the deck. All of the crew were fixed on the water, stuck on the thought that their lover might be down there if only they could bring themselves jump overboard and look or only if that lover would flop its body out of the sea...

As the boy drew near to the heartless captain the man turned, the ships mast and deck creaking with the movement of the captain's arthritic bones as if ship and captain were one.

"Eeeessssst eeet you?" The accent felt like thick wet seaweed on the boy's ear. The boy said nothing and his eyes engaged like snip sights. The captain's face was a skeleton half-wrapped in a slimy flesh. His eyes were gone and replaced by two infinite night skies. His nose was a hollow cavity lined by bone. The captain's bottom jaw had been discarded and his top set of teeth flaunted themselves like rotten piano keys planted in a tar pit. The captain's left shoulder slumped as if it were the face a mountain ignored by God. His belly sank downward as if it were a harpooned whale slipping slowly into a foamy ocean. The boy could not help but stare at the gape in the Captain's chest. Mesmerized, the wriggling white fish fingers of the boy extended endlessly toward the chest.

"Eeeesssssst eeeet you?" The captain asked again. The boy extended farther.

"Eeeeessssst eeeet you?!" The captain throat tensed like a loaded cannon. The boy's fingers felt like astronauts on the brink of a black hole. The experience drove him wild. All things of his past were falling away. He forgot his parents. The boy could not recall the pearls or remember the algae. All that the boy now knew was this moment.

Then the boy, with his fingers near docked, spoke, "I am Solomon Sparrow. I know nothing else. I know nothing of my home or the sea that we are sailing on, but I am curious to touch your heart. If I could I would like to fiddled with the edges of that skin and discover what it feels like."

"Eeeet ees you, then. We haf bean waiting for many years." the captains throat realeased a thin wire of smoke and his body loosened.

The captain took the boy by the hand and walked them both to the edge of the deck. The longing lovers faded from vision and only the boy and the captain stood on the precipice between ship and sea. Beneath them in the water a drove of large lights began rising to the surface like all the lamps of the sunk ships in the ocean. As the lights reached the surface the boy made them out to be a herd of creatures with the skin of jellyfish and the bodies of whales. The creature's light burned brilliant as they rolled their humps out of the water, sliding back in depths like whispers or goodbye kisses.

The boy and the Captain leapt into the water and joined the drove of electric jellyfish whales. Together they swam deeper and deeper and for days and days toward the bottom of the ocean until the reached a single rock carved from the meeting of volcano and water.

My boys, it is here that the very first Solomon Sparrow encountered the heart of the ocean. Beneath this rock there is a single door handle. This door handle is the only one in the ocean. Some of the little creatures in the Pacific will speak of a set of moving doors and fishes in the Mediterranean rattle on about a set of French doors, but this stainless steel ditty in the Atlantic is it. Beneath this door is a heart. This heart is the heart of the ocean. It is the heart that moves the tide, the heart whose pulse pulls the water in and out from the shore. This is the heart that kisses you each time you swim. This heart is the heart that was once ago contained inside the chest of the sea captain who swam with the boy.

The captain reached his boney fingers around the handle and opened the door. A tiny ruby light streamed out into the ocean and filled the boy's eyes. Thecaptain began to explain the heart: "Deees hart eeest me final bait for her. Eeef she does not love mee now then wee are all lost. I geeve me hart to the ocean in eeecks-change for her, for love. But, weee have sea-erched for many years and we have not found love." Two new leaks sprung in the captain's eye sockets.

As the captain spoke, the first Solomon Sparrow could not resist the heart of the ocean. The red glow hypnotized the boy and against the request of the captain and the wishes of the electric jellyfish whales, the first Solomon Sparrow reached his fingers toward the heart and touched it. As he did, the ocean paralyzed. The waters stopped sloshing upon the wide, lazy shores. The fish paused in mid movement. The electric whales gasped as their songs tumbled from the mouths and sank to the ocean floor. The captain was powerless. Solomon Sparrow felt a single sliver of electricity slide up his arm, then across his shoulder, then into his throat and finally the single bolt of electricity nestled itself in the left atrium of the boy's heart. The electric whales gathered around the boy and pressed their chubby noses against him. The boy's arms flung open to the ocean and his body roared with all of the electric whales light. As the bolt from the heart of the ocean began to take root in the boy, the whales poured their light in his bones, veins, liver, and feet. There was a strange light seering withing. This light gave the boy an unruly sense of joy and a wild attack in his spirit.
For ten generations Solomon Sparrow's have carried the heart of the ocean in their

chests and the light of the electric whales in their bones. For ten generations we have searched for and have each sought passion and true love, but with me I fear that our gift has faded. I did not in my 88 years find my love and I sense that all of the beauty of the ocean will begin to die if you do not succeed where I have failed. The electric whales are singing in the deep and you must complete this task.

In each of you I have split the bolt carried in my chest into five pieces and upon my death placed 1/5 of the voltage in your hearts. In your bones I have filled you with the light of the whales. Together you five must now travel the world and revive what has been buried or is being lost as we speak. You must all find love and find it in as many beings of the land and sea as you can. You five carry with all that is left to save what is beautiful and pure and you now must embark on Solomon Sparrow's Electric Whale Revival.

Yours truly and always in love,

Solomon Sparrow XI

Plate I.

ANIS MOJGANI

SHAKE THE DUST

this is for the fat girls
this is for the little brothers
this is for the schoolyard wimps and for the childhood bullies that
tormented them
for the former prom queen and for the milk crate ballplayers
for the nighttime cereal eaters
and for the retired elderly wal-mart store front door greeters
shake the dust

this is for the benches and the people sitting upon them
for the bus drivers driving a million broken hymns
for the men who have to hold down three jobs simply to hold up their children
for the night schoolers
and for the midnight bike riders trying to fly
shake the dust

for the two year olds who cannot be understood
because they speak half english
and half God
shake the dust
for the boys with the beautiful sisters
shake the dust
for the girls with the brothers who are going crazy
for those gym class wallflowers
for the 12 year olds afraid of taking public showers
for the kid who's always late to class cuz he forgets the combination to
his locker
for the girl who loves somebody else
shake the dust
this
is for the hard men who want love but know that it won't come
for the ones who are forgotten
the ones the amendments do not stand up for

for the ones who are told to speak only when you are spoken to and then
are never spoken to
speak every time you stand
so you do not forget yourself
do not let a moment go by that doesn't remind you that your heart
beats 900 times a day
and that there are enough gallons of blood to make you an ocean
do not settle for letting these waves settle and for the dust to collect
in your veins

this is for the celibate pedophile who keeps on struggling
for the poetry teachers and for the people who go on vacations alone

for the sweat that drips off of mick jagger's singing lips
and for the shaking skirt on tina turner's shaking hips
for the heavens and for the hells through which tina has lived

this is for the tired and for the dreamers

for the families that will never be like the cleavers
with perfectly made dinners
and sons like wally and the beaver
this is for the bigots
for the sexists
and for the killers
for the big house pen sentenced becoming redeemers
and for the springtime
that always seems to show up right after the winters

this is for you

make sure that by the time the fisherman returns
you are gone again
cuz just like the days
i burn at both ends
and every time i write

every time i open my eyes
i am cutting out a part of myself to give to you
so
shake the dust
and take me with you when you do
for none of this has ever been for me
all that pushes and pulls
pushes for you
so grab this world by its clothespins
and shake it out again
and again
and hop on top
and take it for a spin
and when you hop off
shake it again
for this is yours

make my words worth it

make this not just another poem that i write

not
just another poem like
just another night that sits heavy above us all
walk into it
breath
it in!
let it crawl though the hallways of your arms
like the millions of years of millions of poets
coursing like blood
pumping and pushing
making you live
shaking the dust
so when the world knocks at your door
clutch the knob tightly
and open on up

running forward into its widespread greeting arms
with your hands before you
fingertips
trembling
though they may be

WHO CAN STILL RIDE AN
FOR THE FIRST TIME

I'm 29 years old and am trying to figure out most days what being a man means
I don't drink fight or love
but these days I find myself wanting to do all three
and I don't really have a favorite color anymore
but I did when I was a kid and back then that color was blue
and back then
I wanted to be an architect an artist an astronaut a secret agent
a ranger for the world wildlife fund
and a hobo
when I was six years old or so I used to always throw my clothes
into my blue and yellow
plastic vinyl
Hot Wheels
car carrying suitcase
and run away
to beneath the dining room table

I've made out with more girls then I wish I've had
and not nearly as many as I'd like to
I've been in love 4 or 5 times
so I doubt I'm gonna try that much more often
and I spend most days making pictures or thinking about making pictures
or masturbating
or thinking about masturbating
and I dream too much and don't write enough
and I'm trying to find God everywhere
trying to figure out this thing He made called a man

and the television set tells me that it's bareknuckled bombing
and if I had a tank or was a movie star my penis would be huge I guess
cuz that's what they keep telling me

and that's what I want cuz that's what being a man means
or least that's what they keep telling me

my pops
takes care of us

he puts the garbage out twice a week

he drives forty five minutes to water flowers

I'm sitting on the bus on Valentine's Day
when a seven year old boy carrying a book of Robin Hood
sits down next to me and asks me my name
Anis.
That's a nice name.
Thank you what's yours?
Quentin.
Anis? Do you wanna read with me?

so tell me what my fists are writing

my fingers open like gates when I type
and the wind is swinging in the wake
motherfucker I lift bridges with poems
and forests grow
in my mother's eyes
I am looking for GOD
Quentin
while this world says fuck you for trying
for this world hates your eyes Quentin
for they are simple and pure
and Quentin
this world hates your fingers
little like the stems of flowers
for not being able to pick up the things you have left behind
because you are still learning to do so

I don't drink fight or fuck but these days Quentin
it's only two out of those three that I don't do
and I've fallen in love 6 7 8 9 10times Quentin so I don't want to want to
but I still do
and I want to find GOD
in the morning
and
in the tired hands of dusk
at the mouth of the river and down by its feet
but instead
I drive sixty
through residential streets
praying to hit children
so that they may stay forever angels
and may stay forever full of night and light and red and crayons
and simple outstretched limbs trying to pick up way too much way too fast
forgetting what it means to be a person
in a world
where egos are measured with tabloids
where automobiles double for morals
where beliefs are like naps
you leave them behind when somebody touches you
and in a place where oil always takes precedence over life
I find myself sitting on a bus watching a small boy float down like fresh
water
carrying a book I used to
asking if I want to share what he sees if only for a little while
and I do
and then asks if I want to give to him what I see if only for a little while
and I read to him
and then says to me he is going to show me the world
and starts reading me the words himself
moving his hands beneath the sentences
not noticing all the time what is written
sometimes skipping whole lines
because his fingers are moving faster then what they are showing his eyes

and I want to tell him
slow
down Quentin

slow down

you don't have to touch and go
you can see it all if your finger whispers on one word

slow down Quentin
and hold what you see just a little bit longer

for you are already holding my attention

and in a world of fast faces
I'm looking for God everywhere
trying to figure out a little better
this little thing He made called a man

I WAS A JAILHORSE TATTOO

your lips are soft petals

that in a past life were knife handles

i can see the shadows of buried switchblades
atoning for their past aggressions in the garden of your smile

your face was a prison yard i was just trying to get shanked inside of

i broke my heart
simply to have you fix it
my fingers long thin stumps from throwing too many punches in the backyard

your God's eyes are the color of glue

my heart is made of wallpaper
i am walking through this house looking for a room that i could make beautiful
so i can stand up against its cleaned walls
and try not to stand out

PEACOCKS

he reads a letter out loud and cannot do so without stopping
his round arms tremble
you can see there are tears being pushed down
the arms straighten
his son watches him
he reads on
of martyrs in Iran dying their numbers increasing day to day

he came to Louisiana when he was 19 to learn how to apply his slide rule
and his ears
when asked if he dreams in English or Farsi he says sometimes both
he has not smelled Tehran in 42 years
he was not there when the revolution dragged bodies with brick and fire
buried women dressed in ash
his son wonders if his father works as hard as he does
as a self imposed penance for feeling like he ran from something
pushing the shovel
to build prayers that stand like shrines
he swings his voice
and stands to the east every day
speaking to God
asking for his Lord to shape him
into something shaped a bit more like the slow glow shoulder of these
drained souls

there are shahs and priests that still scream and weep outside of paradise
for the skulls they skinned
and the piles they made of hair and beliefs
peeled back and scraped bare from bones
his skull is still here
skin peeking through thin soft black hair that he has passed onto his two
oldest
he works harder then ghosts to keep this heart in this world and these

hands in the other
touching doors when no one is looking
searching for poems he buried inside the mother of his children
he sees the pages writing themselves in their faces
he tries not to stare too long
too hard
he may see too much of himself
the birds that he was
carrying islands in their beaks
clutching Persia in their wings
painting their feathers in watermelon juice
he drinks salt
sleeps with his throat open
and waits for these gentle sparrows to fly back inside his mouth
carrying into him the cries of those Persians that no one will know taste
or hear
hymns of what he is
whispers of where he comes from
the gentle memory limbs of his cousins and aunts
pillars of poetry and beauty
holding up Shiraz mighty dome that cut stars down and named them
before melting that silver down into petty bullets and thin wires to tighten
like knuckles
around throats that stood
thick like prayers
spines standing straight as rifles
offering their echoes into the heavens

most nights

he stays up
until he dreams by accident

computer in his lap
falling
asleep on the couch

his sons ride
on gray and black stringed wolves
and beat their drums until their legs vibrate open
carrying souls shaped like the shells of an elephant gun
wondering how to be more
wondering how to curve arms into a cradle instead of a coffin
to hold their father's brow to their hearts
like the beating inside them were the soft warble of the river's current
holding him in the water like a whispering prayer
emptying his rooms
his hands
his shoulders
and setting him into sleep

may his sons pray that when he goes
may the angels
trawl his veins for the pearls that swim inside of them
pulling them to the surface
that God may swallow them softly
and back down into that precious source that they came out from

PANCAKES

i would like to take your heart smoothly out of your breast

some nights i can feel it trembling

like a silent train known by its movement across the midnight rails
a shiver through a child
a dog having a dream
a dream inside a leg of mine
i can feel it trembling while you sleep

i would like to take your heart from out your breast
and holding it with both hands
gently get up from bed
and tip toe into the kitchen
placing it carefully onto the wooden cutting board

then pull a rolling pin from its proper drawer
and began to smooth the heart out
rolling
the pin slowly
back and
forth
tenderly
flattening the soft tissue

maybe turn on the radio at a low level
and hum quietly along
rolling the pin back and forth
my arms constant
moving
like pulling oars
rowing a boat towards you
or like the waves moving beneath me

back
and forth

smoothing the wrinkles out
pressing down

spreading the heart across the cutting board into a wide circle
until it were flat as a pancake

then carefully peel it up
bake it
pour syrup on it
and eat it like one

the whole thing

it makes a large pancake

it is large and perfectly cooked
brown but not too brown with gold amber edges
light and soft in the middle with a slight crisp at its edges
i use my fork and knife several times
it makes many bites
it is sweet and fluffy

when it is firmly inside of me
filling up the spaces of me that were not
i will wash the utensils the plate the board and the pin and the pan i cooked it in
i will wash my hands turn off the lights and head back to bed
i climb in
you stir a little
i pull the cover over us
and hold on-

me filled with a light so heavy

it is the color of gold

and you finally calm
softer
without your quivering heart
filled now instead with a space inside you so wide and dark
you can stretch your legs out
put your hands under your head
and fall asleep
beneath the atmosphere that has climbed into you
spread itself like ink
noiselessly
above your fields
adjusting its wet stars
ever so slightly
to correspond with your eye sight
and as you drift off
their light slowly moves with you

CHURCH

in the broken comma of dawn
i become my father
sleeping rather then thinking
of what i once wanted
my girlfriend told me the other afternoon
"like you"
when i told her
how my pops chooses not to think about whether his life is what he wanted and
what turned out different and
whether his dreams grew fingers and hair or never did
because it would make him sad to think about these things
so he doesn't
like you
you
don't think about your wishes anymore
hope can be a dirty word
and even dirtier when you choose not to use it
i once maybe wanted a house
a red wooden one
with a fence
a hill
a wife
two children
maybe three
maybe one
a stack of breaths to pull and turn through
and a God
that took me in
and kept me warm

THE BRANCHES ARE FULL
AND THE ORCHARDS HEAVY

gentlemen have you forgotten your god?

He weeps out loud
waiting for our dreams to grow ears
while you are making ghosts out of people
making ghosts from your torah
your koran
your bibles

we have shaved our books down
swallowed them
so that the words of God
might flow through us
but the pages just sit in our bellies
speaking to us in dull murmurs as we sleep
a voice
mouthing a sentence so strong and gentle we cannot make it out
...i must   hear you..

we wonder
what to do
make me understand
we wish to become one with our Lord
we hear the voices and think we know what they say
this
this is the word of God
he speaks to me
i hear this i heard it correctly
so we rise
and try to translate the word
with the work

through hearts
we search through thighs
between legs
beneath blankets the bed the needle twist
fuck and the fuck you
curse of the moon
to find You Lord
and follow Your words
but our ears
are too small for our hearts to understand the hum of these songs singing
inside of us

we are trying to decipher the bang buck braille of Your silent throat Lord
but the voices grow and grow fuzzier still
so we stand
and go to the kitchen
and pick up knives to cut the voices out
we stab ourselves
I must hear You
we stab
cutting the flap of our skins
the words twist on the floor of our homes
mixing their sounds with our blood
they drown
but it does not stop
I must Hear You!
we hear the same songs singing in the stomachs of others
so we grab more and more knives to cut those out
but there are more and more stomachs
we need
bigger knives
we need soldiers tanks   missiles
but we still cannot make out the words
I MUST HEAR YOU
we need
dead mothers

children raped from searching
the hospitals are full and overflowing
from us trying to cut our Lord out from our gut
with the blade the pipe
the fingernail twist of the drug
pushed and poked through the arm to the belly
to throw Him up
and in the bang of the scream
we find our savior
the shell in the chamber
is a quiet plea to a distant God
asking for us to be remembered by Him
with the smoke of the tank
through the hymn of the tire
the crunch of the skull
through the babes we bury beneath us
we emptied the tiny shell of their frames
to see if a scrap of our Lord still lingered somewhere inside there
we clutch throats pistols and palms
in the same two handed clasp of prayer
staring into the mirror
we see crypts
fondling the marble of our hearts like they were mausoleums
we are ghosts hungry
for something bigger then what our mouths are kissing

let me SEE You Lord
let me   see You
i am balancing myself
in the middle of the question
beaten by Your hem
black as my eye
i am holding still

so
go ahead

you gentle men of God

you
tender sinners

take your rifles
raise them to my gut
and fire on

hear the song more clearly
do not be afraid to see what it looks like
it does not say what you wish it did

it is too big for us to read even a letter of it
so do not try

instead

cut Him from me

i wish to drape His face with my kisses
and finally sleep softly

THE FISHERMAN

the fisherman throws his nets
at home when he eats
he sits alone
he lights a candle on the table
his plate is round as the moon
he peels the skin of his fish with his fork and knife
peeling it back like a bedsheet
he is always awake before the sun
the fish they do not sleep long
sometimes at night
when he has been drinking heavily
he goes to the rocks at the shore and reads to the fish
he reads to them poems
from books
poems about the human condition
poems about the muscles inside of him that shake and shiver and quiver
question and sleep
he reads
bottle in one hand
book in the other
books clutching poems like they were mothers
afraid to let their children out into the soft fear of the electric night
and he was the wild one to show them this world
his mother will never hold him like that again he thinks
like a little boy
I am too big
book in one hand
and bottle in the other
he reads out loud poems that he hates
ones that fill him with spite
spitting the letters out like bones or like teeth he no longer needed
he stands on the rocks
while the storms fall around him

like a flock of ballooned corpses
he screams
like a drunk preacher cutting a rope
slurring his screams
picking up poems like stones
hurling them at the foot of God's throne
word after word after word
waiting for some door in some black cloud to open up
but nothing happens
the rain falls
the waves swing
the fish sleep
and wake
and sleep
and awaken again and again in the rocking of the ocean
above
he stands like a Noah surrounded by bucket after overflowing bucket
and all he has left
to catch this wet lightning
is this open mouth
so he reads to the fish
he reads to them about things none of them will ever see
about flowers opening
about birds soft as elderly skin large as cliffs
holding heroes between their silver feathers
carrying these men into the open grace of the gods
and into a mighty providence that this fisherman sleeps stands beneath and
inside of
their shields and shoulders
polished hard enough
to blind the sun right back
he empties himself
he empties
and the waves they...
...he goes home
falls into bed

sleeps all the next day
night comes into his window like a fever
like a mother coming to hold him
he wakes
goes to the kitchen
lights his candle
sets the table
cooks his audience
and peels back its skin like a bedsheet
before crawling inside

Plate II.

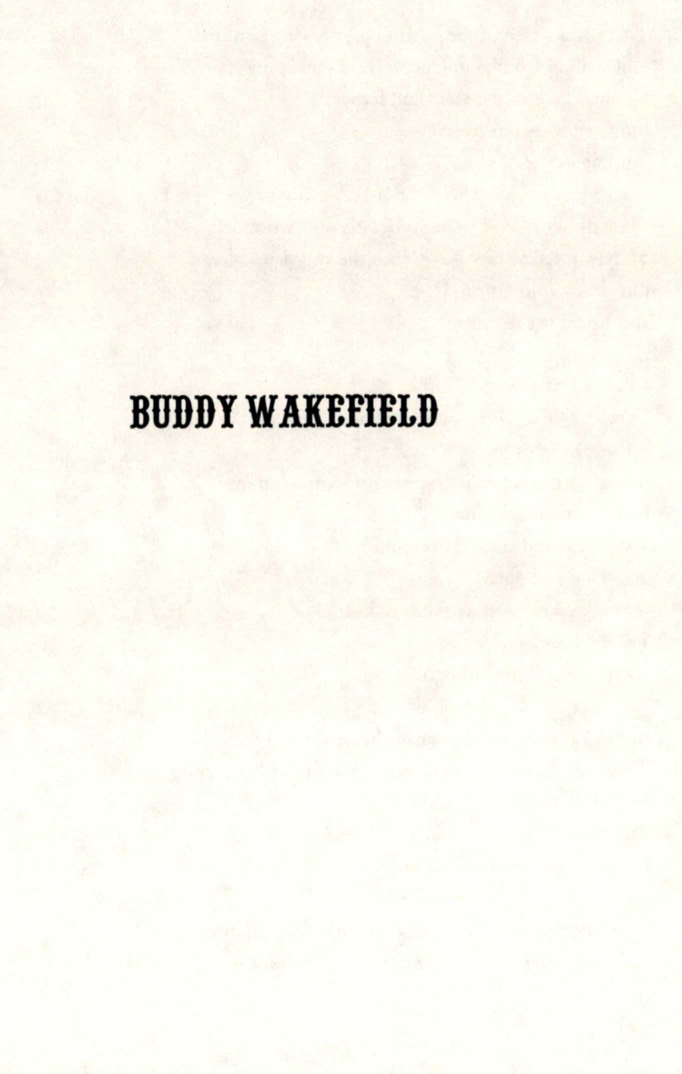

BUDDY WAKEFIELD

BEDROOMS AND BATTLESCARS

As best as I can remember
this is how it happened…

There was a tree in the bottom corner of a corn field
where I hid from people who lived inside my house.
I called them step-sisters and fathers
but they were monsters
holding out for light.
They were people who did not know what they were holding out for.
They didn't intend to be so beastly and wounded.
They wanted to cross over into the way I wander,
but they could not find me,
and I paid for that.

In 1974 I was born.
The next three years were a bit of a blur,
understandably so,
though my mother has repeatedly reminded me
that I was a loud baby.
I wobbled and sucked my thumb
marveled and opened up,
shat my pants, cute as the next kid,
and my cheeks
could be used for sailing.

But in 1978 my mom's car broke down
We were brutally rescued by a truck driver for 8 years.
He had the hell inside of him.
Rug burn.
I know because he pulled me across the floor.

One day my mom decided it was not okay anymore that
he kept falling into other women's – ya know –

vaginas
so we left him, realizing
we had not actually been rescued all those years ago.

In those days
I jumped 6 feet from my light switch to my bed
in order to avoid the hands of anything underneath it.
There are still dents in my shins
because I didn't always hit the mattress.

Bedrooms and battle scars.
both keep well in the dark.
Hard dark.
Paid with uppercut
and heart spark
spark plugs and fist
first
release.

I'd fall in love with you
if you would beat these people out of me.

GANDHI'S AUTOBIOGRAPHY

Gandhi's Autobiography is on my pillow.
I put it there every morning after making my bed
so that I'll remember to read it before falling asleep.
I've been reading it for 6 years.
I'm on Chapter 2.

Gary Necci gave me a book when he left my house one time.
I don't remember the title of it exactly
but I think it was called something like,
"Kid, You Are Seriously Co-dependent."
He thought I might wanna flip through it and learn about that.
I feel like it's more important to finish Gandhi's autobiography first.

I keep forgetting to put "focus" on my to-do list.

I keep forgetting to wander and have fun.

I know I'm transparent
but my insecurities are in all the right places
so go ahead
have a look.

When I was a child I would chase my babysitter around the house
viscerally sounding out the end of the letter "L".

LlLlLlll!
…llll

Have another look.

When will we own ourselves completely?
Tell me what it is you want me to own
and I will take it.

Damaged goods?
You bet
Hit or miss?
No doubt about it.
Misses important social cues?

Yes, I do.

I am dirty underneath the light
pale on the backside of my bright
and feel a little bit stupid about learning a language when I see God
because that guy…
so fast.

My best friend can speak 6 languages.
I still get excited that English took hold.
Sometimes I don't feel like I'm doing my part on this planet.

Sometimes I read without paying attention
hoping everything will just sorta sink in so that
if I ever need the answers – like on a test –
my subconscious will somehow pull through for me.

I talk too much.
If you see me being quiet
don't ask what's wrong.
I'm just practicing.

I often wonder if anyone died because of
the pencil I handed to a prisoner at San Quentin.
He stuck it in his pocket.

The point is
there are things wrong with us.

There are things wrong with me.

But I do have the ability to split epiphanies with my face
on demand.
Hold me like a birthmark. Awkward if you have to.
I wander, so if you lose me, don't worry.

After the big tsunami,
the only structure still standing in the wiped-out village of Malacca
was a statue of Mahatma Gandhi.
I wanna be able to stand like that.
Even after getting gargled and spanked
and spit out by God,
I wanna know
that I don't have to fall every time the sky
opens up like a coin return to change me
just so little lines on maps can draw circles around my blood
to show scar here
in the shape of Gandhi
on my pillow

to show that I have been here before
and this is not the last time I'll see the light.

GIANT SAINT EVERYTHING

There were days I wanted out.
But then You would go and do things
like dive into the Vancouver ocean,
big brilliant cliché poem that You are,
water rolling off Your back
as You swam toward a sunset
that hung like a sacred recipe painted
all the way around Your holy head.

And then there were the ways You watched me
moving back into my cave where the wheels turn,
same wheels that drove You off.
I should have told You
before talking in terms of Forever
that any given day wears me out and works me sour,
that there are nights when the sky is so clear
I stand obnoxious underneath it
begging for the stars to shoot at me
just so I can feel at Home.

What's left of You now is a shrine
built from the pieces I kept of Your presence,
Your incredible stretch of presence.
It sits in Our room like a sandpiper
cross-legged and crying,
remembering the night we met
and the day You left, and the Light
shifting in between.
By the side of it stands a picture of the poem where I promised,
"You will never have another lonely holiday."

The words "I Promise" and "Forever"
begged me not to use them

but sometimes I don't listen to God,
so You can imagine how much it hurt
to let Your last birthday pass
with no word. August 3rd.
You weren't the only one comin' up lonesome.

Listen, if I had to make a list
of everything everywhere
- and I mean everything... everywhere -
the very last to-do on that infinite list of
every – single – thing – would be – to hurt You,
so I need You to know
that in an attempt to keep my promise
I did write a letter to You on Your birthday.

It was covered in stickers of flock-printed stars,
choir claps, and a bonfire of buttercups stuck in the air,
but when I finally drew enough courage
to send You all the Love in the World
my hand snapped off in the mailbox
from clenching.

It was returned to me with a gospelstitch, a hope stamp
and a note etched into the palm I had to pry open
with the pressure of pitching doves
reminding me
we agreed to let each other go.

There is a point when tears don't work
to wash things away anymore.
Grabbing for breath has now broken my fingers.
I miss You so much some days
that I beg for the airplane to crash
with just enough time in the freefall
for scribbling "I Love You" across my chest.
That way – when they find my burning breast plate –

they will tell You how the very last thing I did with my life
was call out Your name.

Arnold Remond Liesting

I know You're momma didn't raise a sissy,
so it's best if I believe
that You've bounced back and been born again,
but, Baby,
in the bottom left corner of dreams
in the dark spot
where it gets windy and hollow
I can still see you flailing,
eating knuckle cake,
full torque and tender,
heart pounding from being pulled under,
feet bleeding from bracing for endings,
tongue dying to curse Forever
because promises murder us backwards
when people like me don't keep them.

And sure, we all deserve absolution,
but especially You. You and Faith,
You've got the same hungerpunch,
same song
still rising off the watertrain running through the laws
of a moon dead set on daylight
digging marbles from the trees
of a Love not scared to make no sense
and monkey enough to see
the same devastating reason for living this life
My Giant
Saint
Everything

Forever

I promise You
these words have buckled my lips
so far back to the beginning
that I am now only allowed Today,
so from my snap-chested heart spraying
fully flying
sending out the birds:

Today I stop believing in words.
Today all my visions reverted blurs
like the night We saw the Light
and I could not shut up

but I swear I was feelin' silence.

GUITAR REPAIR WOMAN

My mother told me,
"If you ever become a rock star
don't smash the guitar.
There are too many poor kids out there
who have nothin'
and they see that shit
when all they wanna do is play that thing.
Boy
you better let'm play."

Okay, if she ever starts in on one of these lectures
your best bet is to pull up a chair, chief,
'cause Momma don't deal in the abridged version.

She worries about me so much some days
it feels like I'm watching windshield wipers
on high speed
during a light sprinkle
and I gotta tell'er, "Ma,
yer makin' me nervous."

She was born to be laid back,
y'all, I swear,
but some of us were brought up in households
where Care Free
is a stick of gum,
and the only option for getting out
is to walk faster.
The woman
can run
in high heels
backwards
while bursting my bubble,

double checking my homework,
rolling enough pennies
to make sure that I have lunch money,
and preparing for a meeting at school
on her only day off
so she can tell Miss Goss the music teacher,
"If you ever touch my boy again, big lady,
I'll bounce a hammer off yer skull."

I remember her doing these things swiftly
and with a smile
in her discounted thrift store business suits off layaway.
She wore them bright and distinguished enough
to cover up the 30 years of highway scars
truckin' through her spine.
Some accidents
you don't need to see, rubbernecker.
Keep movin'
'cause she made it.
She's alive
and she's famous.

We can stretch Van Gogh paintings
from Kilgore, TX to Binghamton, NY
and you still won't find the brilliant brush strokes
it takes to be a single mother
sacrificing the best part of her dreams
to raise a baby boy who – on most days –
she probably wants to strangle.

We disagree - a lot.
For instance, she still thinks it's okay
to carry on a conversation
full throttle
at 7 a.m.
whereas I think…

Oh, wait, I'm sorry…
I don't think at seven in the morning.

But we both agree that
Love
makes no mistakes.
So at night time,
when she's winding down
and I'm still writing books about
how to get comfortable in this skin she gave me,
I see rock stars on stages
smashing guitars.
It's then when I wanna find'm a comfortable chair
get'm a snack,
and introduce them to Daylight:

This is my mother,
Tresa B. Olsen.
Runner of the tight shift.
Taker of the temperature.
Leaver of the light on.
Lover of the underdog.
Mover of the mountain.
Winner of the good life.
Keeper of the
hope
chest.
Guitar
Repair
Woman.

And I am her son,
Buddy Wakefield.
I play a tricked-out electric pen,
thanks to the makers of music and metaphor,
but I do my best to keep the words in check,

and I use a padded microphone
so I don't hurt you,
because sometimes I smash things,
and I don't ever wanna let'er down.

PRETEND

Pretend
On this side
There's an albino monkey
Makin' bass in a jug with'is tongue

Pretend
On this side
There's a pitch black woman
Dressed in a slow tornado
Who looks so much like the night time she almost turns blue in the sun
She's gonna carry us through this tune
With Huntsville, Texas and The Soul-Lifters Gospel Choir
That's my back-up diva

Pretend
Behind me
There's just one
Big
Bang

Now it's you
Pretend yer just bein' yerselves
Pretend you live for a living
Pretend – inside yer skin – you've got a friend who's willing to give you
Everything you ever wanted in exchange for all you've ever been
Pretend you're more obsessed with this moment
And a little bit less with the way it ends

And for a moment pretend
This is a plywood lemonade stand with a sign on the front
It reads:

I got no more lemons

Just my OPINIONS
Yours for a DIME-A-DOZEN today
And they'll always be on the table
But only some gonna set ya free.

Now here's where I'll need you to believe
Please -
Believe that here stands a man who pretends not to fall apart
Who gets so nervous his lips peel back when we give any slack to the dark
Who gets so godsolid scared yer gonnawannatalkabouttomorrowagain
That he'll pretend to stand and listen
With a sharp look on'is face
While a monkey plays
BASS
BASS
With a back-up diva pullin' back-up faith
For this 1-man cross-universe relay race
To try and be more than human
Beginning and ending moment by moment
Rolled over re-birthing again
Because history is repeating itself in record time, y'all,
And we've gotta stop actin' like nothin's happening
When we've got 6 billion dawning truths setting 6 billion different suns on you
But we 6 billion gods are still up-in-arms over what it will cost to follow through
So that YOU can be ME forever my friend
At the same time I get to be YOU
So you can rock me, Brother Rock,
And you can soothe me, Sister Soothe
Like one
Big
Bang

Because I don't believe the big bang really happened yet.
I think a small bang mighta went pfffft
But the big bang is just on its mark
Set

And is really ready to go
Kinda like a slow tornado
Growin' larger than 6 billion words
Movin' faster than a sky flyin' farther away from every square inch of us racing
birds.
It looks a lot like it would if just one brain in the heart of this place rose up
To the actual size
Of the actual voice
It actually contained
Into just one head
Singing just one song
With a word
And six-billion looks on its face -
To see a monkey play BASS
To feel a back-up diva with'er back-up faith
Goin' off
Like one
Big

bang

THE INFORMATON MAN

After over 300,000 miles,
12-dozen breakdowns nervous,
one too many midnights
and a bunch of broken laws later,
I have come here from out of the rain
and into this rest area
caught 22 miles between you and me,
watching the information man
behind his information booth
juggling predictable conversation
with folks who look like iceberg lettuce
and who believe that somehow
the flat lines of small talk will give us life.
I want them to leave,
like a big deal orchestra removing itself from the stringed section
so I can fiddle with fate and make music.

There is a distance the size of bravery.
It forms like words in the mouth of a baby reaching out
for the point where all things meet.
On one end of it sits an information man
who I imagine holds down his second job as church bartender
behind locked doors leading to a bell tower
we will never get to see.
At the other end of this space
I am standing like shoe polish on an overstocked shelf
hoping that one day someone will pick me to make things better.
This is not a showdown or a shootout,
we are not facing off,
but I can feel the rumble between dusk and dawn
as if the chance to come clean with myself
will be outlawed
unless I relax.

I have heard
that if you pull a bent breath
through the second hole of a harmonica
tuned to the key of Georgia
while a train moves by
on the tail end of dusk
there is a good chance
you will finally know
what it means
to rest.
I
have not yet rested.

It takes a long time to make love
with someone who hates themselves.
It feels like I've been standing here
for exactly that long when, at last,
the rain outside drops off
and takes everyone in this rest area with it
except for me, and the information man.

If we were created in God's image
then when God was a child
he smushed fire ants with His finger tips
and avoided tough questions.
There are ways around being the go-to person,
even for ourselves,
but today I will get the answer
and you know what I'm talking about.
THEE answer.
Emphasis on EE answer.

So I put my best foot forward
and pull the kind of deep breath
that gives me away
as someone who deals with anxiety

and odd numbers
every other
other every minute.
In between it
the information man's eyes grab me
then shift
back & forth,
like mopping floors
with the sweat I sweat
in battles against myself.
He's got me locked in and is smiling.

If you've never been rocked back by the presence of purpose
this poem is too soon for you.
Return to your mediocrity
plug it into an amplifier
and re-think yourself
'cause some of us are on fire for the answer.
I am ready for rejection
and rebirthing balance in my stutter steps
when the info guy finally pipes up
like C.R. Avery on a piano box
and says to me:

Listen,
if I didn't have so much of this life all wrong
I would have gotten it right by now.
I talk a whole bunch
but I really only know a few things,
so I'm not saying to follow along verbatim here.
I'll just tell ya the things I tell myself
the things I know
and you can see what sticks...

I know our shoes were stitched from songs about highways.
The best songs are the ones about Georgia

even though I've never been there.
It's the only place I still believe Jesus.

I know that no matter what it is you believe in,
you gotta spare yourself the futility of making fun of God
because that guy hasn't even talked in like…
ever.

I know troubleshooting yourself in the foot
and acting as center of your own universe
is a tricky dichotomy to deal with
but, yes, you ARE the center of the universe.
If you weren't
you wouldn't be here.
So as the middle of space and everything floating in it
it is your job to know
that the emptiness
is just emptiness,
that the stars
are stars,
and that the flying rocks –
fuckin' hurt.
So, please, stop inviting walls
into wide open spaces.

I know everything is out there.
It's why they call it everything.

I know there are times
when you lay your head to rest
you will have a moment of brilliance that grows
into a perfect order of words,
but you're gonna fall asleep instead of painting it down on paper.
When you wake up
you will have forgotten the idea completely
and miss it like a front tooth

but at least you know how to recognize moments of brilliance
because even at your worst
 you are fucking incredible.
It comes honest.
So return to yourself,
even if you're already there,
because no matter where you go
or how hard you try
or what you do
the only person you're ever gonna get to be
and I know it
thank God,
is you.

Eröffnung
Poesia vertice raggiante dell'universo
Anche i tuoi vestiti mortali sono adorabili

Plate III.

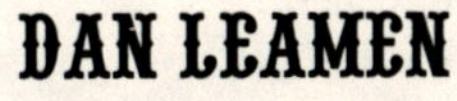

DAN LEAMEN

ALL THAT IS LEFT (THE EMO KID POEM)

Somebody save the emo kids, from themselves,
they are so sad, so very very...ehhhhhh...
because butterflies die and all of the emo boys
and emo girls who wear angst like an antiperspirant
thinking happiness is a disorder involving large pores
and constantly sweating know,
that the beautiful butterfly's little butterfly
heart will never beat its tiny little heartbeats
again and that its pretty little wings
will never again flutter in the breeze.

And think just for a second about all
of the butterflies that die each day and each second,
and how their hearts will never beat again and
how their wings will lay as still as a dead
animal carcass on the side of the road and -
why do beautiful things die?
Because god is a jerk. A big fat jerk. And,

I wish he would stop stealing
butterflies as if butterfly wings are the tea leaves
of heaven, which is where dead butterflies go.
I have to believe that, because yesterday
when I was at this coffee shop where I go sometimes
to cry I was reading some Elliot Smith lyrics
and I spilled coffee all over them this
is life, people spilling darkness onto beautiful things.

I used the sleeve of my black shirt to wipe up
the coffee and discovered that I had ruined a shirt
that is the only color I can see my reflection in
and so I wept a single tear, put it in a jar, and named it:
"hope."

How can you save an emo kid?

Simply kiss a dove,
wrap it in a blanket of navel lint,
and send it out
into a night so endlessly dark that it could only
be an emo kid's soul wedged in the butt crack
of hopelessness.

For each dove you set free
you will receive a picture of your emo kid, crying,
and trying to avoid eye contact with the camera.

You will also receive your very own jar
holding a single tear named: 'hope'.

And finally, a letter from your emo kid reading:
"It is so cold, please send happiness'.

Let the sun beam down like god is peeing.
Let the meadows become overgrown with the lust
of butterflies and let it get so dark
that the only thing left is light.

HOW THE FISHERMAN LOVES

There is the story of the fisherman,
the one in which he longs for what he has lost,
the one in which he chucks
a flaming set of fish heads into the sea.

The burning bundle of slick eyeballs and mouths
left open from their final flops on the steel
deck, is a good luck charm to thicken the next harvest.

Check out his bonanza of glistening hooks, the weight
it takes to sink them and then feast your eyeballs
upon the glowing red heart he has hooked
in the center of his crab fishing cages.

Don't lie.

We would all follow it, fascinated
by that single lit ruby burning in the dark,
spinning with light in a place where fish
are born blind.

He fishes alone, because long ago,
his crew heaved themselves overboard,
all of them pulled by the urge to touch
the ruby, pulled by the urge to touch
what they had lost.

The fisherman stands alone
beard damp, long finger of a pipe extending
from his lips.
"Maybe she is down there."

This is how he has always fished:

an offering of sparkling heads
bellowing in flames, slipping
into the ocean, the wreckage of a tanker,
his chest an open wound,
the sea coating him in salt
as he deposits his heart into the water again.

STILETTOS

Your stilettos keep you out of reach –
precariously steady an ox balancing on flamingo legs.

They were a gift from an antique store
of anti-feminist heirlooms. You were fascinated.

I told you that they had once been used
as spits for men's hearts so you wore them

on a night like all others
men's hearts swelling as if attraction
were veins drying into this single reservoir
your stilettos primed to puncture the skin of the dam.

Men understand love as a rush and you
rushed us only away from that we stumbled home
staying close, my chest open.

You had refused the parachute I had
offered to you, a gift from an antique store
of safe loves. Love is not safe, in your bed
you eased your stiletto into my heart into
a soft lake of blood, a soft place to fall.

THE AMATEUR CANNIBALS FIRST DATE

On the top of my dresser,
the bones kept in a box
carved from a mannequin
I used to nibble on.

Practice.

It is not I am
no longer hungry.
I miss your touch.

On our only date I only fiddled
my filet mignon.

What disgusting normalcy.

I wanted you and you
took my hand like a vulture.
I had never felt such heat slide
of my knife accidentally easing
along your -

blood drizzled over a favorite dessert
our feet pitter-pattering
back to my apartment.

We spilled onto a pile of skeletons
not yet hung
in the casket of my closet.

Dirty laundry.

"Ouchies," you said.

"Yes," I said.

Our bones clanked together out of tune
thumb tambourines on the fingertips
of socially awkward gypsies.

Skins spent the night swirling like the scarves
of uncoordinated belly dancers.

Your fingers
were the most exhausted of our troupe.

I gnawed them off,
one
by
one.

"Yes," you said
as I bit into you
with the savage mechanics
of lust.

"Is this – ," you asked,
"a listing body crashing
into an iceberg of teeth,
hull sucked into a sea of blood?"

Love is complete consumption
blood, skin, hair, teeth,
all dissolving in another's guts.

THE ASTHMATIC BILLBOARD

Beneath the loose curtains of your skin there
is a theatre show spinning chaotically lifting,
trapeze artists flipping into the air.

Long ago you were a damsel
with sweet legs, a dancer long

but now you are a body, heart caught
at the exact moment of break, a juggler
who refuses his queues
pours gasoline onto your rib bones,
and then swipes them in the sizzling
notes still lit in your lungs as he dazzles
the air with a dangerous interpretation of love you
now lack control, your arms meat being flipped
to lions feet.

In the second act, a woman gulps
down knives, licks on a bloody lipstick climbs
up out of the orchestra pit of your throat,
and kisses you with her wounds.

By the arrival of the finale the heartbroken dancers
refuse, anchor themselves in dressing
rooms littered with discarded skins of feather boas.

Once bright and constant, drawing
crowds in tux's, monocles, sleek dresses, you,
your heart is now an asthmatic billboard blinking
in gasps of electricity advertising the exhausted
heat of a body, your body tired of performing.

THE BEARDED WOMAN

The Bearded Woman in her tent, vanity
in front of her, cushion rimmed
with rubies and flat from hours of grooming her
heart a collection of struck matchsticks tossed aside
by the careless flicks and disregard of fire breathers.

The bullies of paper cuts, razor blades balance
on her chin light as tight rope walkers heavy
as lion tamer heads in the mouths of lions, she thinks
everyday of pulling the blades across and shedding
her novelty.

Heaps of freshly hairless cats lay about licked
clean for hours, a woebegone effort to get
it, to finally understand what it is to be smooched
by her, to be lip-licked with the wet muscles
of two salmon lips flopping upstream, dressed
in grizzly bear get-ups.

Tonight, she spent another evening at the end
of the ferris wheel ride waiting for the desperate,
starved lips of lovers dissapointed by another kissless return.

In exchange, The Bearded Woman takes guesses
at the wiehgt of those exhausted lover's
in the arms of the next one to say: "Yes,
you. You are the one I want," and everyone

leaves floating, hearts smoking, blood
a fog, love is an apparition or at least
it is the feeling of cuddling with one.

Imagine us up there, the ferris wheel

paused precisely with our carriage at the top,
the sky, the black coal of it, the single moon
and her valleys like shading in a sketch. Imagine
the thin rings of sound, tin bells lifting
their voices up to us, knees and theighs pressed
againgst one another, our hands damp, our lips wet
and beardless.

THE ENDLESS DISTANCES

Lost in the water longing
for rescue, our raft at best shoty
bamboo frayed our single sail wrought
with holes for seagulls to coast through
when showing off you wondered
if we would ever again see land.

I stared into your eyes into the endless
distances of desire an old sea Captain
eyeballing the sea for the fish
who drove him to madness, I am

sure that your eyes were fully capable
of being this fish.

Fumbling a response I reached into
our supply of coconuts and said, "Longing,
we say, because desire is full of endless distances."
You laughed. There was nothing better
to do and passing a halved cantaloupe into your hand
I felt the gentle buzz hum of lust fall between us
on our skin like seaweed, wet.

I don't know if it was the sea or being
stranded, but everywhere there was distance
and it seemed as if this were what we had set
out to discover.

Our skin sashayed curtain-like in the air, bones
vibrated, an ocean of stranded beaver's teeth
chattering for a shoreline of trees, muscles flirted
with the tensing and untensing of awesome gymnastics,
and all of this, all of this

until our mouths capsized into the waters of our lips
We French-kissed like St. Bernards.
And our fingers shipwrecked on an island of misfit sex toys.

From our wreckage we constructed bookshelves
and stocked them with exhausted copies of the Kama Sutra.

The pages dripped, spines limp, we
had spent all of our lives reaching for things
that were reachable and now, now we
were extending legs and bodies into only the endless,
whatever took us so long to get here?

THE VOLCANO

For years their people had lived
at the base of the volcano.

Of course there were always rumblings
about the volcano spilling it guts,
the great gape in its center oozing
as the earth belched out the letters of the apocolypse.

There was a boy and a girl
who lived amongst the people.

They met during a class for villagers
who were interested in running from the magma.

There is no simple simulation of a volcanic eruption
that doesn't result in a crisp village or toasted
forrest, so they mostly spent their time in class
chatting and watching film of other volcanos bubble and burst.

This is how they introduced themselves:
her warm hand extending toward his cheek,
his mouth packed with all of the hot things
he had wanted for so long to tell someone.

Bored with watching the stock
footage of villagers screams suffocated
by falling tufts of ash, they ducked
out of class one night and headed
for the lip of the volcano,
both saying: "I am so tired of not seeing anything real."

Once there, he dug his fingers into the soot
and carved circles around her eyeballs,

"these dark motes will keep the light
in your eyes from scorching me," he said.

She had lost count of the exact
number she had convinced to come
here all of them desiring to actually
see the volcano and to actually be with her.
She had nudged all of them into the magma.

Her search for a lover ended always like that.

I dare to say it was hot.

The boy pulled his nerves from his guts,
a magician producing another scarf from his mouth
and fashioned a hammock for the two of them to nap in.

She draped it over the crater.

The hammock's blood dripped
with the wussiness of a thousand kitchen sinks
until it crinkled in the fire, exploding
like the wings of gunpowder
moths who flew to close to the volcano's single flame.

The earth began to rattle,
the shaky tension of a first kiss,
his lips fiddled with the edge of hers.

Her hands fell around his back, below
the villager's mouths opened. They were all so close.

TOAST

More than I want to eat some toast,
I want you to love me.
I have grown weary
of sitting in lonesome meadows,
dropping flower petals to the ground
like the pitter-pattering of our heartbeats
sneaking out of doors on cold
August mornings.

I want to wear your orgasm
like a jacket.
I am cold and you are hot
like a polar bear on fire
on a toasty day in the armpit of a sauna.

That doesn't make sense.
I don't care.
Love never does.

Love tells me that I have a flux capacitor
on my toilet
and I can take back all of the shit.

I want you to shipwreck on my bed.
You look like driftwood.
I don't mean that. I take it back.
You look like something valuable
that also survived the crash.

We are just being tossed about.
It's been said before, but I'll say it again:
our hearts are leaky
boats and love is a pile of corks

in a locked room below deck
or some kind of ancient Hindu god
with eight thousand hands
and lots of thumbs.
I want your thumbs to plug the holes in my sternum!

I want to spell your name wrong…
so you can spell it right.
I want to tell you things that may or may not be true,
like: "I can make breakfast."

I want the leaves to fall wherever you walk.
I want the sun to set in your presence
like it is bowing to a more beautiful grace.

I want to go back to the fourth grade and kiss
you behind the brick wall
where my first kiss was set free like a bird
whose broken wing I had spent my childhood mending.
I want to kiss you like that…
like pouring hot chocolate
all over my face
or running a marathon backwards while levitating,
because, when my lips beach
on yours like two drunk sea otters,
I say: "Physics, lick my sauce!"

I want buildings to stand
still and grow monolithic in your radiance.
When you sleep
here, I want the morning to forget
itself and stay awake
all day. I want to rub sand paper on our skin
so we can feel soft again.

I am falling off of oceans.

I am taking in breaths that feel like desperate
tree branches beneath the snow.

I am falling always in love with you.

I am a banished captain of soul
left by my crew of scalawag
broken hearts on the island of your breast
and left with only a pistol and you
are the only smoke signal I want to pour
out of my mouth, the only steel I want to break my jaw,
the only bullet I want to taste on my tongue.

Plate IV.

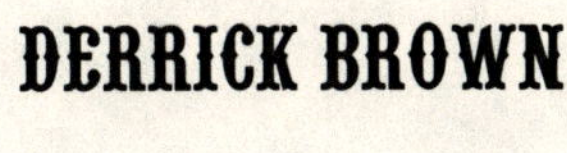
DERRICK BROWN

ALL DISTORTION, ALL THE TIME

Teased by success
we are like vampires in a tampon factory.

It doesn't have to be that way.

Someone plug my lungs back into the guitar amps!
More distortion ladies!
All distortion, all the time.
More overdrive!

Aren't you sick of being appraised wholesale?
Aren't you sick of sailing on listing ships?
Aren't you weary from playing cellos with ex-lover's bones?

I want a piano that will not warp outdoors
when the rain demands slow dancing.

I want to skew the difference between Tai Chi and Chai tea,
and end up drinking a tall glass of graceful force.

I want to lick my hands after I touch someone that has just become
razzle dazzled in the breasts.

I want birds to come close enough to hear them speak Aviation Spanish.

I want your record collection in my throat,
and my thumb in the electric ass of the all night jukebox.

I want my shoulder blades mounted in the museum wonderful of the fantastic
knives.

I want church in a bar. I want to pass out and hear you say Amen in that bar.

I want a skeleton night light in the closet.

I want your wow in my now so we become NWOW.

I want free shit to not cost anything.

I want to roar brightly like a disco ball of fish-hooks
so you can hang on my words and I can spin in your small miracles of light.

I want my kitchen to be a Brazilian dance floor
with a pot of your sweat in the oven
and a fridge stocked with butt lust.

I want new sheets. I'm gonna need 'em now.
I want your silver muscles cut into a quilt. Let me sleep under your strength.

I want more pony lamps. No reason.
I want to sing this into all tail pipes until I'm exhausted.
I want to smell everything.
I want to remember that the sky is so gorgeously large,
I feel stranded beneath it.
And when I gasp,
I only want to gasp for more.

BARNEY SHEEHAN LIVES FOREVER

Two tired Americans stumbled through the stone streets
of Limerick Ireland.

Our money dissolved.

The books beat against our backs in our rucksacks,
heavy as the great castles in the skyline,
the ones fighting off renovation.

The Irish breeze chased us into every pub and we sat and drank slowly until we
forgot we were cold.

My jacket
was lost
or floated away drenched in Swiss river water, British gasoline and German wine.

Who knows what black angel spent the night on guard
teeth chattering
eyeing my jacket
until she caught my head and laid me in the cobbled gutter gently
and removed it as payment.

In the morning bus, the fields raced us
a blur of flared gold and swinging emerald light,

We were starving for new epic territory.
Beauty swallowed us in Ireland and Barney Sheehan, a former jockey with hell in
his veins and sainthood in his heart
turned us into family.

We were living off the kindness of strangers and drink tickets and long embraces
and conversations of religion and death grazes.

He showed us the pride of Limerick with the bright energy in his vinegar tongue.

"Now boys, do ya want some eggs boys, Oh sure ya do, sit down and eat it up, go
on, you know I ran for mayor once, I woulda been absolutely fantastic, I would.
eat those eggs now! Cmon ya skinny little… I'll smack em down your throat,
what do ya want to do boys, oh I'll tell you. Were going to see the city is what
were going to do. Now cmon, you're not done eating, Oh I…"

The streets of Limerick were coiled like a sea monster.
My Pal walked as fast as Chicago and kept up with Barney's amazing pace better
than I.

I stopped him and said I may never ever see this place again
so I need to take it in and walk real slow.

Barney Sheehan took us to the white house pub,
where the people listened as if it mattered and that night
it sure felt like it did.

In the window, he had hung an Irish flag and next to it,
An American one.
We thanked him and it felt appropriate to hug him.

"We're all the same. Everyone in America is Irish. You're home. Consider your-
selves home, boys."

The poetry and beer was incredible.
You could feel the words wedge right into peoples chests.
This was Limerick,
far from the soft girls in Dublin that
danced with us in a boat house until the sun bolts came on.

Far from those who will join the ranks of the wonderous and the vanished.

Far from Long Beach California.

Barney gave us a perfect tour later until a mesh of starlight fell across the island.

The streetlamps guided us through the tendrils of Limerick.

Cars whispered somewhere.

The soft hills were inhaling the night. Morning dropped all over us,

Barney showed me my Brown family crest and something inside felt ancient and
my blood struggled towards the page, to try and touch it.
It felt like I had never had a history until that moment.

It is fair to say that Barney gave me history.

The next day, I went to river in a noon as overcast as wool.

The choirs of Irish rallying around me with the great acidic jesting that only the
Irish can do well.

A country with an arm spanning west held me as still as the Lake of Innisfree.

The small tide came to me and loosened the soil.

Near the middle of the lake, two swans, one moving fast, the other slow.

The meandering and focused one, the drifting swan moved on to somewhere,
a glimmer in the wings
We are treading.
I wondered about Barney and what good words meant to his life.
I found this poem:
When You are Old
When you are old and grey and full of sleep,
And nodding by the fire, take down this book,
And slowly read, and dream of the soft look
Your eyes had once, and of their shadows deep;

How many loved your moments of glad grace,
And loved your beauty with love false or true,
But one man loved the pilgrim soul in you,
And loved the sorrows of your changing face;

And bending down beside the glowing bars,
Murmur, a little sadly, how Love fled
And paced upon the mountains overhead
And hid his face amid a crowd of stars.
-YEATS

Barney
I do not know when I will return to Ireland
but I promise I will return...
and every poem you speak forth
 I hold
as small promises
that you will live forever.

BEYOND THE CLEARING, A SOUNDER OF BOARS

through the curtains of night oak
and into the clearing out back of my house,
the sounder of boars returned.

snouts along the ground swaying like metal detectors,
tusks as white as shards of prison soap
they advanced, steadily

tuskless sows grunted cadence
as piglets swung their stripes from the tree line
and into formation.

the sounder crunched through the flakes of autumn like a new search party,
to surround my home.

they do this every year.

 at first i appeased them with acorns and candied pecans.

time passed and i moved on to confrontation.

some spears i kept in the coat closet behind the vacuum.

i scattered those bloody bristles, but scared them for only a season.

another year and the sacrifices continued
small turtles and a wristwatch placed in the clearing.

i tried offering rabbit last year. they dragged it impaled from my porch.

sliding back beyond the clearing, they marked my land with the hare's mess.

this year was different.

i waited it out for days as a hostage and they remained in a circle.

i filled with anger.

the remaining spears were weak shots. my arms trembled from lack of nutrients.

the last of my food was a half-skinned deer, a small buck from a summer hunt i
kept in the garage freezer.

this night i carried it to the porch and wished i had a phone
or a wife
or neighbors
or friends with guns.

i offered the young meat to them. they remained staring at my eyes and did not
approach.

"what do you want from me?"

nothing.

"do you want me to come with you?"

the long boar surrounded by the others patted a hoof at the ground.

"can i pack my things?"

the boar snorted goop onto the soil.

"can i write a letter?"

the boar squatted onto his belly and the others followed as dominos.

so i came back inside to tell whoever find this…this.

i don't know if you should look for me.

if you do, i couldn't take any of my stuff.

i am probably beyond the clearing
through the oak
in a most beautiful ending.

MY FIRST CPR CLASS

We met at a CPR class for singles.

We learned that the inhalation phase of breathing
is called inspiration.

She said, "If you breathe into someone else,
it should be called something more magical."
I said, "Like expiration?"
She said, "Something more spiritual."
I said, "Resperado."

We met at a CPR class for singles.

We both showed up early for the poison healing chapter.

During drills, I volunteered to choke.
She volunteered to Heimlich me.
Her tense arms reached around me like a semi-heterosexual cowboy
and pulled hard.
I coughed out a Tic-Tac from the day before and told her it was a tooth.
She said, "Your teeth smell minty."
I said, "That's the nicest thing a non-dentist has ever said to me."

We met at a CPR class for singles.

She was all dressed up in blue emergency.
Styled in the symptoms of shock.
I wanted to tell her some poetic madness,
a vagina wrangling phrase like:
"You are a swinging peppermint nightstick of pink,
crashed on all my horny bionics."

All that came out was,

"Hey, isn't it funny how old people really love pie?"

She said, "Isn't it beautiful how old people respect every breath.
We breathe 17 times per minute."
I said, "Less if sleeping."
She said, "Less if kissing."
I said, "And um, or… snorkeling?"

We practiced mouth to mouth on the dummy.
She said she was used to making out with the brainless.
She dropped her gum in its mouth as a joke… for me to find.
I had a hard time retrieving it with my tongue.
I got it after five minutes.

The instructor suspended me from further oral interactions
with all plastic devices within the room.

When it came time for a live volunteer to mimic an unconscious stroke victim,
I beat her to it. I laid down.
She stepped up and I closed my eyes.
I liked her mouth, docking upon mine in its Armenian grip.
I felt upon my lips, her 'I might look like a cop in 24 years" mustache and knew
we had something in common, and that something was justice.

I moved her down to mine.
We kissed like Europeans who just discovered that it's O.K. to put ice in a coke,
The gum fell into my throat and I actually choked.
The instructor thought I was getting into the drill again and kept the class coming.
 A dude with a beard made of tuna fish, breathed into me like a diesel leaf blower.
A nineteen-year-old girl with a goiter and no upper lip breathe-sneezed into me
wetter than an whale porno.
Then a short, spandexed man who looked like Boris Yeltsin's dead baby
slobbered into my tonsils until he pressed his gold ringed hands on my chest
and the Big League Chew rocketed out like a geyser.

We met at a CPR class for singles.

I learned that a mouth finding another mouth
in it's desperate gaping,
could land and surrender to shared air,
and the thing that passes between mouths as the lips connect
could save your life.

…that and massive pumping on the breasts .

THE VICTORY EXPLOSIONS

I try to remember my youth.
It evaporates into 76 memories.

One memory was that you believed
the earth was made perfect by God,
and that humans fouled it up
and that sin was something we gave birth to,
as God shook his head at our idiocy.
"How could they choose terror and loss?"

I don't think God really ever wanted perfection
if he designed the things he made with an instinct to screw up.

Fighting it and sometimes failing is beautiful and hard.
Screwing up is part of the program. Call it sin. Call it human.
Maybe there are codes built inside of darkness needing light
and vice versa.
 It did not shake your belief in the existence of a God,
but it shook your belief in the bland necessity for perfection.

It birthed the belief that
the human who could figure out
the balance of a hunger for winning and a deep respect for losing
would win the life trophy.

You go back to the first year you learned to daydream in a clothing rack.
The first year butterflies bloomed adrenalized
in your wet guts.
In the 5th grade you tempted everything.
Bicycles spinning,
the smell of girls,
pencils at war,
dismantled radios.

Launching off the swing set into the air, your first sensation of flight.
An innocent season for getting your ass kicked by a boy
who thought it would be a nice sign of his love.

Adam White heard I'd kissed her underwater at her Dutch pool party, French
style, which is weird for a 5th grader.
These were skill sets as a 5th grader; my tongue was not prepared for.
I did not know who started the rumor,
but I was about to pay for it with the cash of my face.

The same field we chased girls together in,
the strong, freckled Adam challenged me to my first fistfight.
I felt like a coward in a costume of a coward.
I was skinnier than a dead model.

No matter how much I denied the rumor,
his freckles kept popping from his face like brail.
"You're ass is grass, Derrick Brown."

I know.

The crowd gathered.
I stared at them like a sparrow
trapped in an airport terminal,
wanting the sky but stuck against the glass.

I stood like a cricket in a junkyard of fiddles
unable to stop my legs from shaking music from my knees.

He swore he loved her, and that I would pay.
His forehead blistering
wrinkling like a crumpled valentine.

Where in the hell were the teachers?
What I wanted was mercy.
But even I didn't know what that word meant.

His fist came out and crushed at my jaw.
My eyes went black and all that I saw
was a shower of lighting bugs.
Children flashing into sunshine.
My teeth penetrating my cheek.
 Falling backwards,
blood fertilizing the softball field.

But instead of freezing, I stood up again.
He struck me down, once more.
Eyes, ricocheting against the back of my skull.
The earth, meeting my failure, legs buckling,
skin reeking with contact,
and I stood up again.

And he socked me with all his might.
 Matchsticks lighting in my cheeks.

And I stood up again.

And he hit me so hard my Mother's eyes bled.
And I fell again, and I stood up again, and again, and again, and again,
until he grew tired of socking me and left. Everyone left.

Alone there, baptized in warm blood,
I now knew the cost of the satin sponge and slop of a girls ridiculous lips.
Cause guess what?
We did kiss under water at that Dutch pool party
like aqua spies
 and it was worth it.

There's nothing for me to learn from winning.

It is losing that has yielded the unforgettable lessons.

Losing is pregnant with chance.
Victory escorts loss to every dance.

Harmony,
harmony.

THE KUROSAWA CHAMPAGNE

Tonight
your body shook
hurling your nightmares back to Cambodia
Your nightgown whisped off to Ursula Minor.
I was left here on earth feeling alone,
paranoid about the rapture.

Tonight
I think it is safe to say we drank too much.
Must I apologize for the volume in my slobber?
Must I apologize for the best dance moves ever?

Booze is my tuition to clown college.
I swung at your purse.
It was staring at me.

If I beat you
I hope I only beat you
to the bottom of the bottle

We swerved home on black laughter.
Bleeding from forgettable boxing.

I asked you to sleep in the shape of a trench
so that I may know shelter.

I drew the word surrender in the mist of your breath.
Waving a white sheet around your body.

'Dear, in the morning let me put on your make-up for you,'
loading your gems with mascara
then telling you the truth...

I watched black ropes and tears ramble down your face-
Lady war paint.

A squad of tiny men repel down those snaking lines
and you say
'Thank you for releasing all those fuckers from my life.'

You have a daily pill case.
There are no pills inside
It holds the ashes of people who died
            ...the moment they saw you .

The cinema we built was to play the greats
but we could never afford the power
so in the dark cinema
you painted pictures of Kurosawa

I just stared at you like Orson Welles
getting fat off your style.

You are a movie that keeps exploding.
You are Dante's fireplace.

We were so broke, I'd pour tap water into your mouth,
burp against your lips
so you could have champagne.

Sparring in the candlelight

Listen-
the mathematical equivalent of a woman's beauty is directly relational
to the amount or degree other women hate her.

You dear, are hated.

Your boots are a soundtrack to adultery

Thank God your feet fall in the rhythm of loyalty.

If this kills me, slice me julienne
uncurl my veins and fashion yourself a noose
so I can hold you once more.

COME ALIVE

Citizens of Narnia,
I must admit
I was a reluctant candidate for Mayor.

I have shaken the hands and hooves of many
through out this great land.

and I must admit
for many, the beat inside has died.

A great sorrow overwhelmed me
for even the drums in my chest
were growing quieter each day.

When did we become a library of children ,
shelved like great novels
no one had time to read?

As Mayor of Narnia
I declare that this day must be the day we come alive.
I will declare a day for dipping our hands in butter
so we can practice letting go of what we were
and watch our hands emerge as telephones
so we can know our calling.

brrrng. it's the future. it's for you.

As mayor of Narnia,
I will declare a day of common sense-
on behalf of waiters everywhere.
If you can't tip 15-20%
Then you don't get to go out to eat.
To the centaurs on a fixed income, this goes for you too.

As Mayor of Narnia
I declare a day for talking to the trees
What are they saying? They're saying climb me,
carve your future lovers initials into my spine,
sacrifice me for your books.
Every book, every page is my blood. I give this to you.
If it's a war for the lands of imagination, I am ready to die.

Go ahead- get young on this day.

We're gonna build a big dumb blanket fort to keep out the cynics
and if you get hurt in the construction
we have a reindeer in the lobby that will hold you and talk it out
(there there)

We are gonna Invite snow angels to the bonfire
and give them Smore flavored popsicles.
cause they love it

I declare a day for Buying cereal with the worst nutritional value˅
but the biggest prize.
Go meet your prize.

Go somewhere and sing the genitals electric
We will champion the crushed.

We're gonna fly kites in reverse
with the sail planted firmly in the soil
and our bodies on a string
sculpting clouds into the faces of people we miss.

Were gonna make thank you cards
And rest them on soldiers' graves.
Were gonna raise a hand
in the back of the world classroom
and the answer we come up with

is to pull the night down
Stare stars in the face
and reclaim lost wishes.

We're gonna capture the details.
We're gonna turn off the machines.

To the working class
We are not the dishes we pass.
We are the passion we dish.

If you've been away from Narnia for awhile, welcome back.

The kingdom is outside.
The kingdom is inside.
Today is the day we come alive.

HOT FOR SORROW

When the police helicopters showed up
I grabbed onto the skid
and they flew me crosstown
to your house
where you slept
like jewelry in a coffin

I screamed out:

I don't want to be the best lover you've ever had
I just want to be your favorite.

File me under hot for sorrow.

When I couldn't find your picture, I ate unwanted videotape and dreamt.
When you appeared, soft-focused and outlined in lasers,
embarrassed of your little T-Rex arms and seaweed hair,
we danced on the ceiling like Lionel Richie on Meth
until it was time to walk you home from naked class....A+.

This crosseyed sniper
misses you so much.

The heavy solo night music of the city
tells me what is buried beneath:

Ambulances hooked on one ballad.
A sky turning red over its opponents.

Night melodies of helicopter switchblades
slice through this city.
The noise tells me there is still crime down there.
5000 air machines cannot stop crime.

5000 searchlights cannot stop crime.
5000 police fully moustached, with a John Wayne box-set, our names on every
baton,
cannot stop crime.

I now know that what I feel for you is crime.

This is why I like the sound of police choppers:
Not because it makes me feel safe and watched over
but rather because it is the music of war
and tonight, love
they were playing our war.

Plate V.

MIKE MCGEE

FOR THE BIRDS (AT 3:33AM)

I sat out on her balcony
There was a bird sitting near the table
Maybe it was injured
Maybe it was dying
It seemed to be comfortable with my presence
Maybe it fell
And was just waiting to die

I began to cry over my cigarette
As the bird listened
Stalling on words that just won't come out at 3:00am
Tears for the bird
Tears for her
Maybe just sweeping the weepy feeling away
Cuz deep down I know
I too have fallen
And now I'm just waiting to die

Joy always seems to come when she sleeps
When I'm ready to tell her everything
Three cups of coffee in me, and a thousand words later
She dreams of a place where she can be she
And maybe I'm there with her
Maybe I'm not
She seems to be comfortable with my presence
But certainly there is a place for her
And right now she's just waiting to fly

GEEZ, US!

I was hanging out with Jesus the other day
He had just gotten beaten up by some pro-lifers
He called them anti-lovers and wished them luck
He was wearing a Gandhi mask when it happened
He had originally planned to wear a Thomas Jefferson mask
but nobody knows who that guy is anymore

We drank some grape Kool-Aid on His balcony
and watched the sun go down beyond Los Angeles
I asked Him what it was like to die
He said it was His favorite out all of His Dad's art projects
Death is so quick compared to life
because it's just that awesome

I asked Jesus what He liked about today
and it took Him too long to respond
I dozed off and dreamt of four men on Shetland ponies
riding around, breaking windows
They were the Four Midgets of the Apocalypse
They burned down miniature golf courses
and stabbed people below the waist

Jesus woke me up and presented me with an omlette
which was delicious!
As any evening breakfast would be
when made by the Son of Man

I told Him that He seemed like the cool older brother I never had
He thought that was cool and asked me to stop masturbating so much

I told Him that everyday I feel a certain sense of unexplainable lonliness
he said it was because I spend too much time alone
I pondered that for a moment while He topped off my Kool-Aid

His apartment was decorated with film posters from movies
that told His story in some way
Last Temptation Of Christ
Jesus Christ Superstar
and Repo Man
Willem Dafoe signed one of them
He spoke well of Willem Dafoe
But He didn't own a DVD player or the DVDs in order to watch those films
I asked Him why and He said
that most of them are misunderstandings of His life
and the rest of them pretty much suck balls

I had the feeling that the human part of Him wants to be forgotten
but the Heavenly side is anxious to introduce everyone to His Dad
I asked Him why He moved to L.A.
He said it was the hidden beauty
That having to search for the good
meant that when it was found
it had to be authentic
He also pointed out that L.A. is one of the few places
a man dressed like Him in public can still go unnoticed

We watched Mexican television
and He interpreted all of the game shows and soap operas
It was late and He said I could take the couch
which would have put Him on the floor
I took the balcony instead

In the morning He woke me to another omlette
this time wrapped in a big flour tortilla
I wasn't hungry, so He wrapped up and put it in a bag
He said I should eat it later
then He asked me to shave His head
I felt uncomfortable
He said it was okay
and that His strength came from somewhere else

He just wanted to fit in with the rest of us

I shaved His head
and wandered home
Later that afternoon, while riding the bus with L.A.'s maids
I noticed one of His hairs stuck to my collar
If I had a girlfriend, and she found it before me
she might wonder who it came from
but I don't
and she can't
and so she won't

I just sat on the bus and wondered to myself

I pulled out the breakfast burrito
and birthed it from its aluminum foil
I noticed a face burned into the tortilla
a simple accident or miracle for me to enjoy
I immediately knew I couldn't share it with anyone else
I wondered how often Jesus
promoted himself on food items
The Lower East Side in New York gets a new Starbucks
East L.A. gets a Jesus statue
that cries and bleeds French vanilla flavored coffee creamer

I ate my Jesus burrito neck first
and smiled once I realized
that it was actually the face of Willem Dafoe

GOING YOUNG

Death to a child is not a quick, passing thought. There must be a course in medical school that teaches doctors and nurses how to tell a person they're going to die, let alone a child.

When I was a child, I had certain medical annoyances that sent me to the hospital pretty often. The year I was born, I was diagnosed with Spina Bifida. A birth defect that ranges in severity with each patient, but most are far more serious than mine.

In 1985, at nine years old,I lived in the children's ward at Walter Reed Memorial Hospital, in Washington DC. I met a nurse from Texas. He was in his mid-20s, 6 foot something, black, and nothing like any of the hundreds of nurses I had met before him. He would change my diaper, feed me, bathe me, and hold my hand when the doctors needed more blood from my already tapped veins. His voice was outstanding and it would boom when he got mad, but that only happened once, and I'll get to that later.

You see, his voice was built from singing – choirs, choruses, and just spontaneous songs for all the kids at Walter Reed Memorial Hospital in Washington DC. This man always seemed to do what was right, no matter how it looked or sounded, if it felt right to him, then it had to be done.

He laughed at my jokes and said he couldn't wait to see me on TV someday, because he knew I'd make it out of there. I was only nine years, and maybe he said the same thing to all of the other kids in my ward, but he sure made me feel like I was one of a kind. He encouraged me to be funny and broaden my skills. He devoted most of his time to the kids that weren't going make it out – all the ones lying in their last bed. He would sing for them all the time and just sit near them when they slept, so that they would have him to wake up to; the next best to mom and dad.

Sometimes, I would get jealous because he was my only friend, and yet I had to share him with the other kids. Most of my peers were my age, but had little, baldheads and weighed half of what I did. When I asked my friend why they looked this way he said, "Cuz they're special. They get to go home early."

I knew what he meant; I was a devout Catholic with no fear of heaven, but my friend assured me that the one thing he had to look forward to everyday was a certain sense of fear from all of those kids. So, to get away from the torture of chemo, radiation, tests – and the fact that most of their siblings didn't come to visit cuz it was just too hard to bear seeing them that way – these kids would get away from it all by going to the children's playroom. A room full of every imaginable toy and game donated by the healthy children of all the doctors and nurses of Walter Reed Memorial Hospital in Washington DC.

Personally, I avoided the children's playroom.

On one beautiful day, my friend came in just to check on me. I was alone in my room, and he asked where the other kids were, and I said they had all gone to the play-room. He asked me why I hadn't gone with them and I said, "Cuz it's depressing." He stared at me for sometime then said, "No, that's depressing." He said, "You got something these kids don't. A future. These kids are gonna get all their birthday presents early, just in case. You make all the nurses laugh, but you don't share it with the people who need it, and that ain't right." His voice boomed like never before. He was so mad at me. He left the room and I didn't see him for three days, which is impossible in a hospital. I stayed in my bed that whole time, wondering if he would ever come back. When he did, he came armed with a wheelchair, and without saying a word he put me in it and wheeled me down to the playroom.

I sat before a room full of the unhealthiest children I'd ever seen. Kids that should be adults right now but aren't. My friend leaned into me and whispered, "Please, make them smile. I know you can do it." He announced to the crowd of bald kids that I had come to perform for them. They all turned to face me and waited.

My friend the nurse left the room and listened down the hall. All of the children at Walter Reed Memorial Hospital who weren't bedridden were there. I can say with assurance that they did smile, the whole room smiled and laughed at everything I did. The entire hospital could feel the energy from those kids. They enjoyed themselves like there was a tomorrow.

I can't remember anything I said or did, but there is nothing in the world better than a room full of the happiest children in the world, children who have every reason not to smile or laugh, or enjoy themselves. Some of them smiled for the last time. That was my first audience ever. It was surely the best audience I will ever have.

I can only hope that anyone of those children find me someday. Just know that what you went through keeps me going.

My friend the nurse was right and so here I am. Never again will I avoid a playroom, especially the one at Walter Reed Memorial Hospital in Washington DC.

I'M NOT... BUT IF I WERE

I'm not thin...but if I were...
I'd be the thinnest man this side of the NBA
I'd wake up each morning with a smile on my face
and I'd sing songs in the shower by Skinny Puppy and Thin Lizzie
as I lathered up into an emaciated frenzy
I'd be thinner than thin
I'd wear a skinny tie to work and drink decaffeinated coffee with skim milk
I would be a thin bastard!
No! I would be the thinnest bastard!
looking for other thin bastards to give a bony handshake to
And me and my thinness would travel the world around
spreading joy and celery
And I would call up Brad Pitt
just to say, "You've put on some weight!"

The world would love me if I were thin and they'd want to be thin right along
with me
I'd teach them all how to be thin with my thin handbook
We'd do thin things and eat thin things, while going to thin places
And when one of us saw something we liked, we'd get the skinny on it!

But I'm not thin
I've been hit on by more overweight people than I have thin people
Maybe they know something I don't
But for now, I don't need to be thin
and I'm cool with anyone who is

I'm also not gay...but if I were...
I'd be the gayest man this side of San Francisco
I'd wake up each morning with a smile on my face
and I'd sing show-tunes in the shower
as I lathered up into a homosexual frenzy
I'd be gayer than gay!

I'd wear a rainbow tie to work and drink coffee with my pinky out
It would be a gay pinky!
No! It would be the gayest pinky, looking for another gay pinkies to give handjobs to!
And me and my gayness would travel the world around
spreading joy and condoms,
and I would call up Brad Pitt
just to say, "Come OUT and play!"

The world would love me if I were gay and they'd want to be gay right along with me
I'd teach them all how to be gay with my gay handbook
We'd do gay things and eat gay things while going to gay places
And when one of us saw something we liked, we'd say, "That is so gay!"

But I'm not gay
I've been hit on by more gay men than I have straight women
Maybe they know something I don't
But for now, I don't need to be gay
and I'm cool with anyone who is

I am, however, Mike McGee...
and because of this I am the best Mike McGee I know
I wake up most mornings with drool on my face
and I sing my own songs in the shower as I lather up into a Mike McGee frenzy
I'm Miker than Mike
I don't wear a tie to work and I say, "Fuck coffee!"
Fuck latte, fuck espresso, fuck Starbucks, fuck you, fuck me...which rhymes well
with Mike McGee
and me and my Mike McGee-ness should travel around the world
spreading joy and leftovers
and I would call up Brad Pitt
just to say, "Smell It!"

The world doesn't have to love Mike McGee and no one wants to be Mike McGee
with me, but I could teach you all how to be me with my Mike McGee Handbook
and we would do Mike things and eat Mike things, while we're at my house
And when one of us saw something we liked, we'd say, "Smell it!"

I am Mike McGee and I've never been hit on by Mike McGee
Maybe I know something I don't
but for now I don't want to be anybody else
cuz I'm cool with Mike McGee...Smell it!

I am Mike McGee and I've never been hit on by Mike McGee
Maybe I know something I don't
but for now I don't want to be anybody else
cuz I'm cool with Mike McGee...Smell it!

SOUL FOOD: A DUEL WITH DEATH AT LUNCHTIME

So last week the Angel of Death comes knocking at my door
Totally interrupting Perfect Strangers
And I'm like, "Dude, you are so early! There is so much more I wanted to do with
my life!"

"You've had plenty of time for that!"

"You know, you sound a bit like Sean Connery."

"No, he sounds a bit like me."

"Whatever, dude. There's gotta be some sort of loop-hole. What if we competed
for my soul? Like some sort of contest."

"I love a good challenge. If we can both agree on one, then the winner may keep
your soul."

At this point I remembered I had a pot a ramen noodles waiting for me on the
stove. The Angel of Death was lured into my kitchen by the sweet aromatic joy of
powdered shrimp flavoring. I could see that Death was hungry, so I made a second
pack of Ramen. We sat and ate in silence, but my hunger just wouldn't subside. So
while I raided the fridge, I noticed Death scoping my Rice Krispy Treats.

"Still hungry, dude?"

"We'll take one for the road." he said.

And we both put a Rice Krispy treat in our pockets.

"Actually, I could probably eat half of all your food."

"So could I, dude, so could I."

And it hit us both at the same time. We pulled out every bit of food in my house and divided it all into equal halves. We had one rule: First person to finish eating their half of food keeps my soul.

We sat down on the kitchen floor surrounded by an odd buffet. The world's greatest food challenge began. But this was no ordinary match.

I took an early lead as Death fumbled opening a can of refried beans. I plowed through a dozen eggs and half a gallon of milk. I strategically swallowed spoonful after spoonful of leftover lasagna, without chewing. Death caught up to me with a tub of butter and half a soggy pumpkin pie. I hustled my way through cans of corn, green beans, kidney beans, chili, chicken soup, fruit cocktail, and a few cans of peas, but I was stopped dead in my tracks by a mystery can. It's label missing and nowhere to be found. Damn, dog food! No time to think, I had to eat it.

Death was now ahead of me by two-cans of beer, a frozen steak and what we think may have been tamales. I burped to make room and continued on in the feast for my soul. I ate broccoli, cauliflower, cucumbers, oranges, bananas, a container of baking powder, two cups of salt & pepper, a jug of Pepto-Bismol and a can of whipped cream. We reached our last item of food. One. Raw. Potato. Each. We slowly gnawed our way through the raw potatoes, swallowing our last bites at the exact same time. It appeared as though we had a draw. Then Death looked to me with a sly grin and handed me a Tupperware bowl with my half of uneaten Jello. I grabbed a straw and sucked it down, saying:

"There's always room for Jello, bitch!"

But Death just smiled and said, "I believe I finished my half before you. Your soul is mine."

But I just outsmiled him and said, "What's that in your pocket, hooker?"

His face sunk as he reached into his pocket and pulled out the last Rice Krispy Treat.

He looked to me with fear as I handed him my wrapper, and swallowed a mouthful of crispy, marshmallow goodness. "I believe I win, fucker."

With that, the Angel of Death bowed and vanished.

I sat down to an episode of Full House and ordered a pizza...
cuz there's never anything to eat at my house.

THE SMILE

I'm sitting in the break room at work. Just outside the door is a window to the street. Anybody who walks by said window can see me in said break room.

As I ate my toasted Asiago bagel with cream cheese I lamented the fact that I had to return to work. Outside of the break room were grumpy ass customers just waiting to yell at me and my nametag.

I continued eating when this woman walked by the window, made eye contact with me and smiled. Not a "what're you looking at" type of smile, more like: "Hey there sad eyes, take this smile from my lips. Let not this day bring you darkness, but a new light and harmony. Let thy peace be done."

It was a "Shine on you crazy diamond," kind of smile

I was awestruck by her power; she went by at the speed of modern humanity. It would have been easy to miss her noble gift as she passed me by. Being a stranger, I assumed she could only smile at chubby white men with bagel crumbs in their goatees. It is possible, however, that when our eyes met…she farted.

But that singular smile was salvation from a seemingly sucky day. Like a virus, she passed to me this simple contagion of contortion.
My face was paralyzed into a position of positivity–a smile so solid you'd swear I lost my virginity in the break room twice to Milla Jovovich wearing nothing but Scotch tape. This was beyond sexual bliss, this was me being giddy on a Monday at work thanks to a stranger on the street. She compelled me to pass on a smile doubly-wide to everyone who came before me. I left with my co-workers smiling like they'd just won a year supply of cake, milk, and weed. There I was, this giddy, pear-shaped genius, smiling so hardcore my gums were bleeding. My mission of mouth mechanics had me making mad men merry, while working wildly to wow women to wonder, "Why the fuck is he so happy?" AND "How do men that chubby get so damn cute?"

I'll tell you how…Smiling is sexy, and I smile all the time. I am cute because I still believe smiling is the first step we can take toward helping out one person at a time. Even if I didn't have teeth, I'd still smile, because teeth are an unimportant aesthetic in the diplomacy of smiling. It's almost better than eating a free buffet dinner with a stripper at a casino where you just won 300 bucks on a silver dollar you found in the gutter. Almost.

Abraham Lincoln didn't smile and look what happened to him

Smiles are the last proof and truth that we are beautiful, that we can do more than we believe ourselves capable. A complete stranger smiled at me, and although my life didn't attain perfection, it did get a little better. It's as if she said, "Baby, I know how you feel, and we'll get through this." Her smile carried me throughout my day and later that afternoon I stepped into a coffee shop where I usually buy orange juice, but instead I asked the girl behind the counter if she would have dinner with me sometime. She said and nodded yes, punctuating it with a smile. It caused a revelation to smile across my brain as I realized I had never asked a woman out before and that made me smile.

FINIS

COME AND MEET US.
WE'LL TOUCH YOUR FACE.

www.electricwhale.com

Printed in the United States
142452LV00001B/125/A